Singapore Math
Grade 1 Workbook

Get your child excited about learning with activities suited for Grade 1.
Your child will build foundational skills in addition, subtraction,
comparing numbers, measurement, time and geometry.
Our workbook will help your child practice the skills they need to
succeed, while making learning a positive experience .
Also give your child the chance to refresh their memories and sharpen
skills with games and challenges.

Activities, Challenges and Brain Games.

Table of Content

Adding with Pictures

Count and Add.

Adding with Pictures

Count and Add.

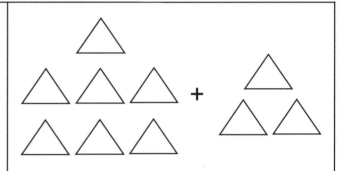

□ + □ = □

□ + □ = □

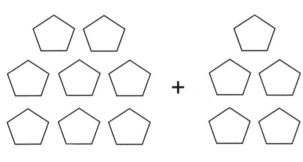

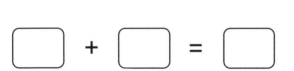

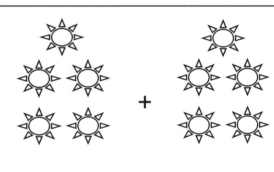

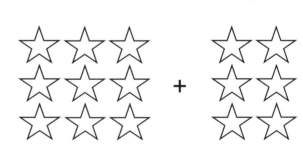

□ + □ = □

□ + □ = □

Adding with Pictures

Count and Add.

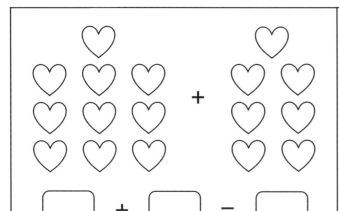

☐ + ☐ = ☐

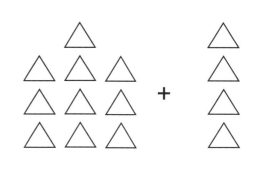

☐ + ☐ = ☐

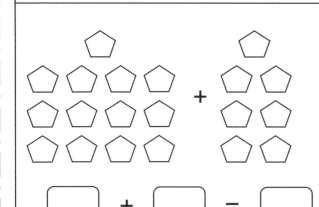

☐ + ☐ = ☐

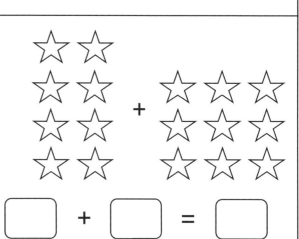

☐ + ☐ = ☐

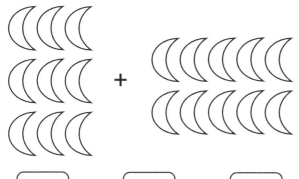

☐ + ☐ = ☐

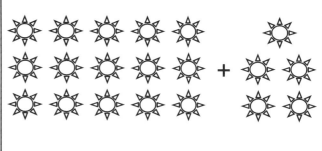

☐ + ☐ = ☐

Adding with Pictures

Count and Add.

Use your math skills to find the value of each "?".

🐃 + 🐃 + 🦊 = 5

🦊 + 🦊 = 2

🐃 = ?

🦊 = ?

🐓 + 🐸 = 3

🐓 + 🐓 + 🐓 = 3

🐸 = ?

🐓 = ?

Game and Challenge

Use your math skills to find the value of each "?".

+ + = 6

+ = 4

+ = 6

= ?

= ?

= ?

Addition in Columns

Find the sums.

2 + 3	4 + 1	5 + 2	3 + 4
2 + 6	3 + 3	4 + 2	5 + 3
2 + 2	7 + 3	4 + 4	5 + 5
8 + 2	6 + 3	9 + 1	2 + 7

Addition in Columns

Find the sums.

7 + 4	6 + 6	3 + 9	7 + 7
5 + 9	7 + 6	8 + 3	5 + 7
4 + 9	8 + 7	9 + 6	8 + 8
6 + 8	8 + 9	7 + 9	9 + 9

Addition in Columns

Find the sums.

10 + 3	14 + 0	22 + 2	11 + 7
13 + 2	45 + 3	36 + 1	51 + 8
62 + 2	55 + 4	77 + 0	83 + 3
94 + 4	88 + 1	70 + 7	60 + 5

Addition in Columns

Find the sums.

1 + 10	4 + 14	3 + 20	5 + 42
6 + 60	4 + 55	7 + 81	6 + 71
2 + 93	7 + 70	8 + 61	5 + 73
9 + 90	8 + 80	2 + 91	1 + 81

Addition in Columns

Find the sums.

11 + 10	14 + 12	13 + 10	12 + 15
13 + 14	11 + 11	17 + 11	10 + 10
19 + 10	12 + 12	13 + 13	13 + 16
17 + 12	14 + 14	18 + 11	15 + 14

Addition in Columns

Find the sums.

35 + 11	41 + 23	62 + 35	18 + 71
27 + 52	73 + 21	55 + 20	60 + 33
84 + 14	66 + 11	91 + 00	80 + 10
33 + 33	51 + 41	44 + 44	72 + 27

Mental Addition

The numbers in the circles added together makes the number in the linking rectangle. Find the missing numbers in this puzzle.

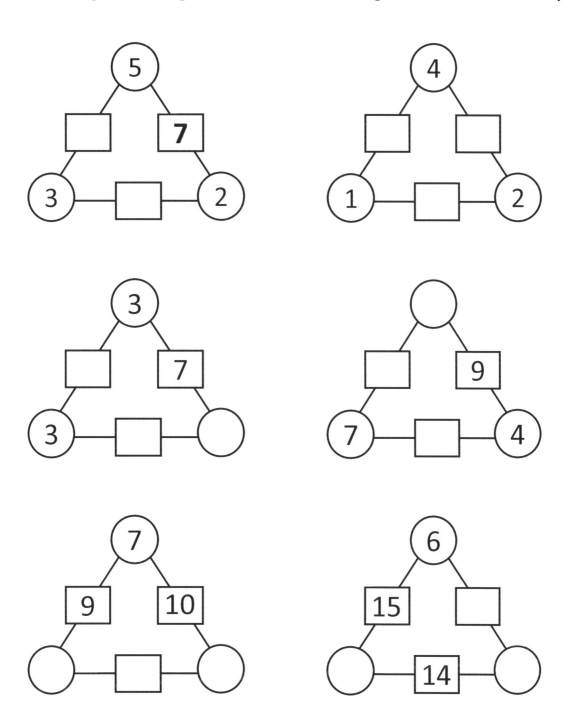

Mental Addition

The numbers in the circles added together makes the number in the linking rectangle. Find the missing numbers in this puzzle.

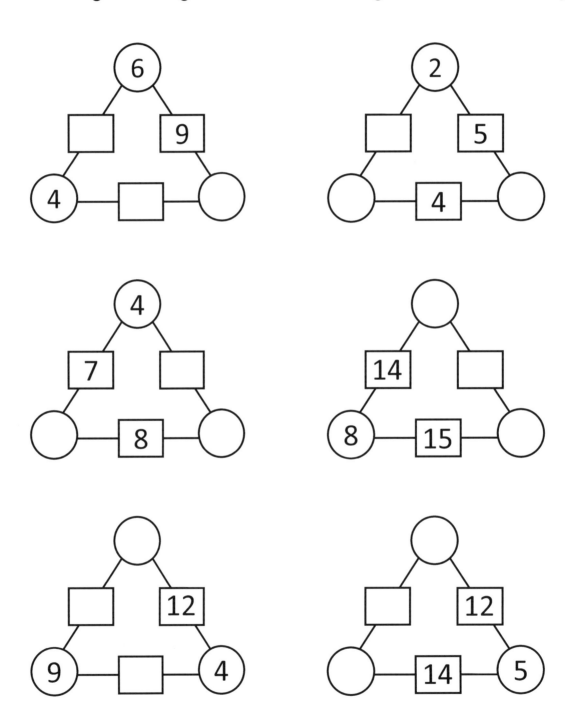

Mental Addition

The numbers in the circles added together makes the number in the linking rectangle. Find the missing numbers in this puzzle.

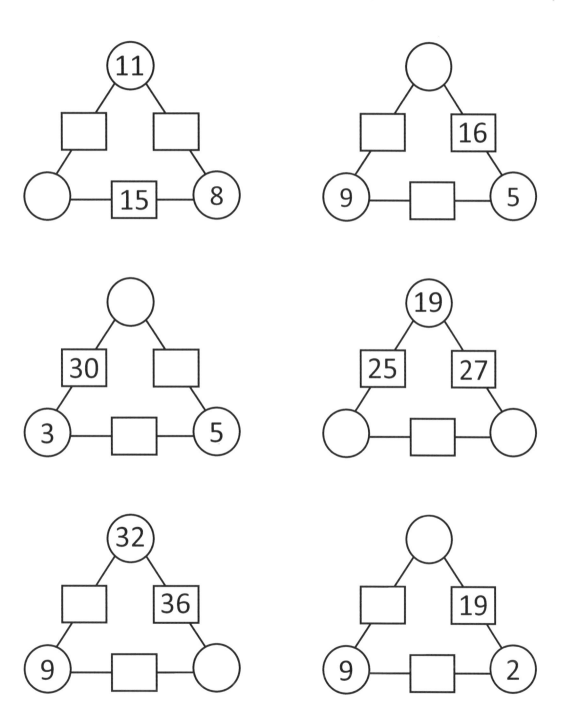

Mental Addition

The numbers in the circles added together makes the number in the linking rectangle. Find the missing numbers in this puzzle.

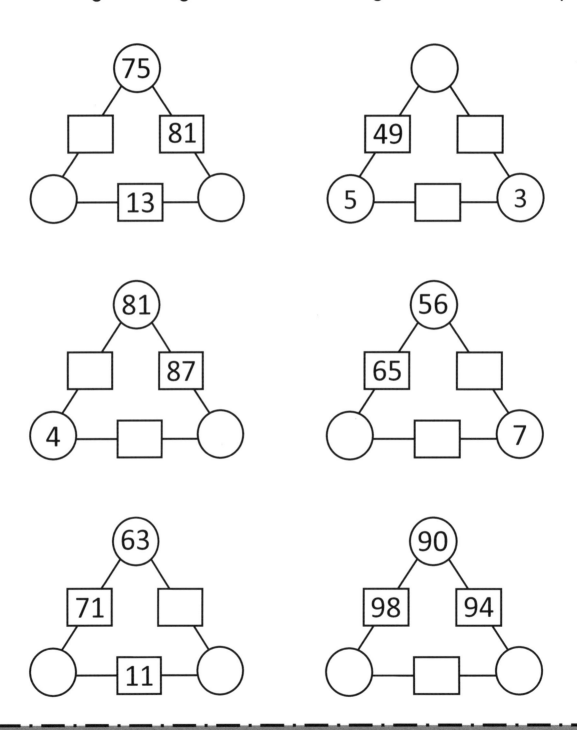

Mental Addition

The numbers in the circles added together makes the number in the linking rectangle. Find the missing numbers in this puzzle.

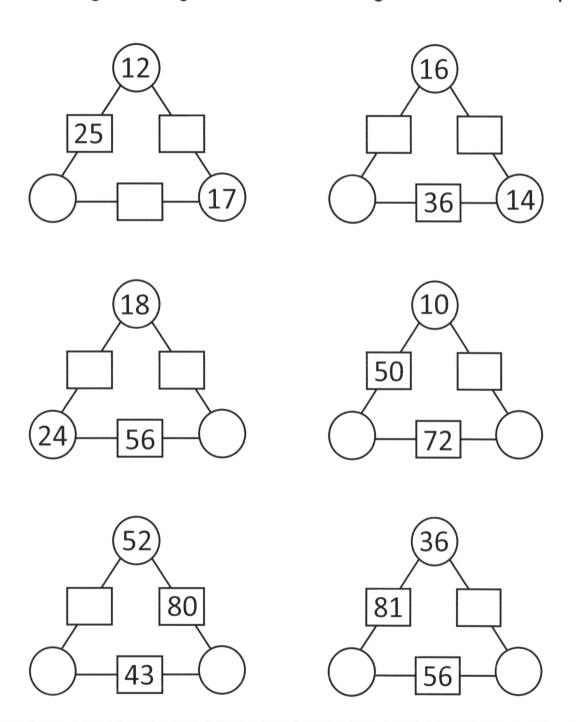

Mental Addition

The numbers in the circles added together makes the number in the linking rectangle. Find the missing numbers in this puzzle.

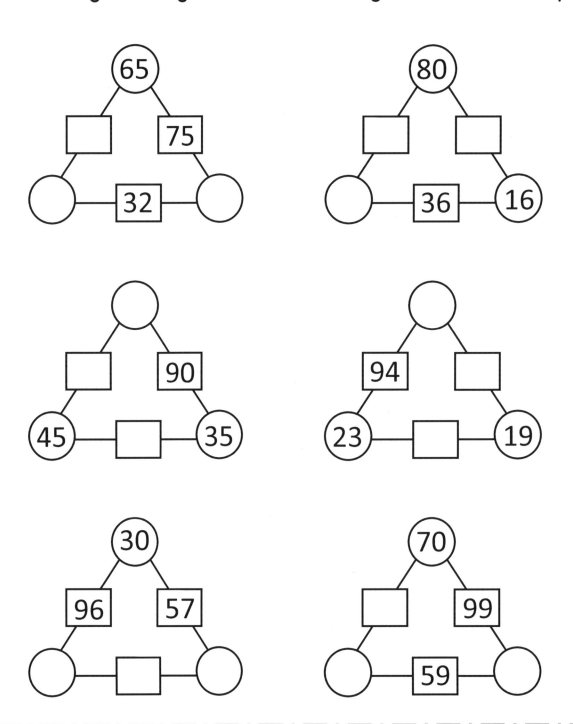

Making Numbers

Think of five ways to make 6.

Example

$3 + 3 = 6$

$2 + 2 + 2 = 6$

$\boxed{} + \boxed{} + \boxed{} = 6$

$\boxed{} + \boxed{} + \boxed{} = 6$

$\boxed{} + \boxed{} + \boxed{} = 6$

Think of five ways to make 5.

$\boxed{} + \boxed{} = 5$

$\boxed{} + \boxed{} = 5$

$\boxed{} + \boxed{} + \boxed{} = 5$

$\boxed{} + \boxed{} + \boxed{} = 5$

$\boxed{} + \boxed{} + \boxed{} = 5$

Making Numbers

Think of five ways to make 8.

☐ + ☐ = 8

☐ + ☐ = 8

☐ + ☐ = 8

☐ + ☐ = 8

☐ + ☐ = 8

Think of five ways to make 7.

☐ + ☐ + ☐ = 7

☐ + ☐ + ☐ = 7

☐ + ☐ + ☐ = 7

☐ + ☐ + ☐ = 7

☐ + ☐ + ☐ = 7

Making Numbers

Think of five ways to make 10.

$\square$ + $\square$ = 10

$\square$ + $\square$ = 10

$\square$ + $\square$ = 10

$\square$ + $\square$ = 10

$\square$ + $\square$ = 10

Think of five ways to make 15.

$\square$ + $\square$ + $\square$ = 15

$\square$ + $\square$ + $\square$ = 15

$\square$ + $\square$ + $\square$ = 15

$\square$ + $\square$ + $\square$ = 15

$\square$ + $\square$ + $\square$ = 15

Think of five ways to make 12.

$\Box$ + $\Box$ = $\boxed{12}$

$\Box$ + $\Box$ = $\boxed{12}$

$\Box$ + $\Box$ = $\boxed{12}$

$\Box$ + $\Box$ = $\boxed{12}$

$\Box$ + $\Box$ = $\boxed{12}$

Think of five ways to make 20.

$\Box$ + $\Box$ + $\Box$ = $\boxed{20}$

$\Box$ + $\Box$ + $\Box$ = $\boxed{20}$

$\Box$ + $\Box$ + $\Box$ = $\boxed{20}$

$\Box$ + $\Box$ + $\Box$ = $\boxed{20}$

$\Box$ + $\Box$ + $\Box$ = $\boxed{20}$

Addition Word Problems

Read and solve the problems.

1) Three birds were sitting on the fence. Five more birds came to join them. How many birds are sitting on the fence?

2) Four toucans are sitting on a tree limb. one more toucan joins them. How many toucans in all?

3) Linda ran four miles on Monday, three miles on Wednesday, and ten miles on Friday. How many total miles did she run that week?

Addition Word Problems

Read and solve the problems.

1) Catherine bought 2 candies for 7 cents and 3 bubble gums for 11 cents each. How much did she spend in all?

2) Sara made 7 Rice Krispie Treats. She used 9 large marshmallows and 12 mini marshmallows. How many marshmallows did she use altogether?

3) Lucy ate 4 apples every hour. How many apples had she eaten at the end of 3 hours?

Addition Word Problems

Read and solve the problems.

1) Emma saw four bugs eat five flowers each. How many flowers total did the bugs eat?

2) Isabella bought 3 pizzas. Each pizza had 9 slices. How many total slices of pizza did she have?

3) Benjamin read 2 books per day. How many books did he read in one week?

Addition Word Problems

Read and solve the problems.

1) Jack, James and Gianna are keeping score of the game they are playing. When a player wins a game, that player gets 5 points. If a player loses a game, the player has 3 points taken away. If it is a tie, every player gets 2 points. Jack wins the first game. How many points does Jack has after the first game?

2) Amelia gave 3 pieces of candy to each student in the group. The group had a total of 11 students in it. How many pieces of candy did Amelia give away?

3) Each CD rack holds 20 CDs. A shelf can hold four racks. How many total CDs can fit on the shelf?

Game and Challenge

Use your math skills to find the value of each "?".

jug	+ umbrella	+ flower	=	19
rocket	+ rocket		=	10
jug	+ rocket		=	9
flower	+ jug		=	12

rocket = ?

flower = ?

umbrella = ?

jug = ?

Game and Challenge

Use your math skills to find the value of each "?".

yak + fox + yak = 17

fox + goat + yak = 15

+

yak = 21

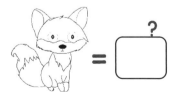 = ?

 = ?

goat = ?   fox = ?   yak = ?

Game and Challenge

Use your math skills to find the value of each "?".

👟 + 👗 + 👟 = 30

+

☕ + ☕ + ☕ = 18

+

☕

=

20

👟 = [?]   ☕ = [?]   👗 = [?]

Each of the integers from 1 to 9 is to be placed in one of the circles in the figure so that the sum of the integers along each side of the figure is 19.

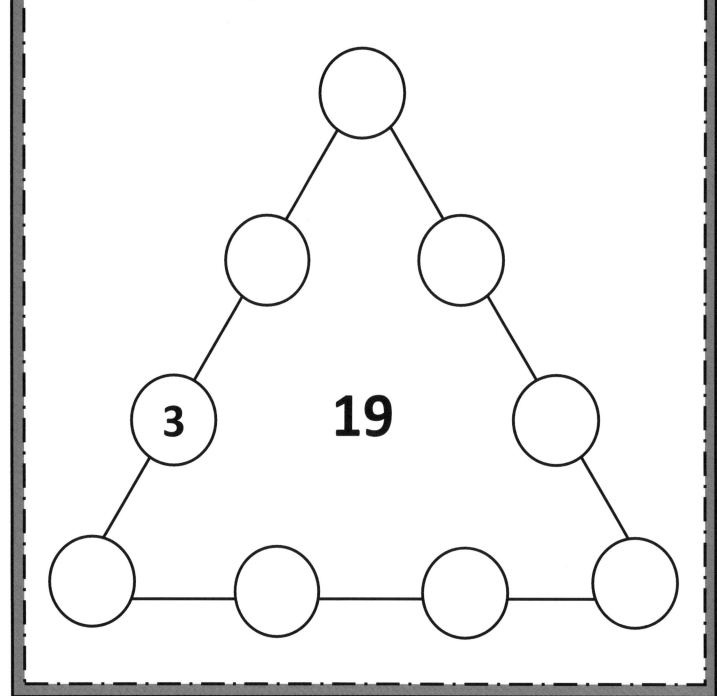

Each of the integers from 1 to 9 is to be placed in one of the circles in the figure so that the sum of the integers along each side of the figure is 20.

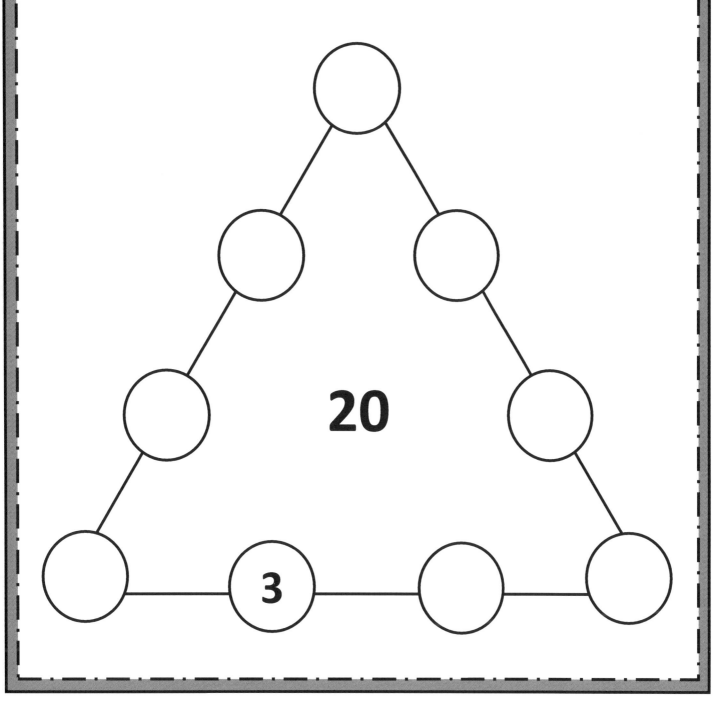

Subtracting Using Pictures

Count and Subtract.

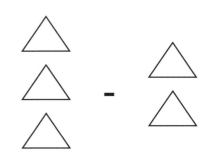
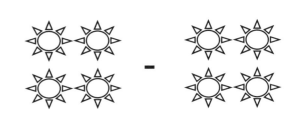

☐ - ☐ = ☐

☐ - ☐ = ☐

☐ - ☐ = ☐

☐ - ☐ = ☐

☐ - ☐ = ☐

☐ - ☐ = ☐

Subtracting Using Pictures

Count and Subtract.

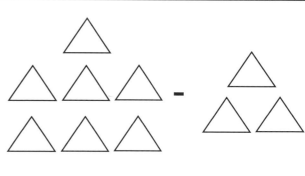

☐ - ☐ = ☐

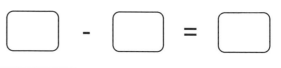

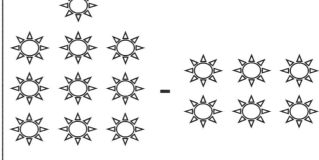

☐ - ☐ = ☐

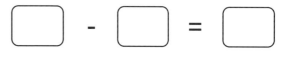

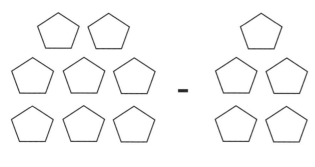

☐ - ☐ = ☐

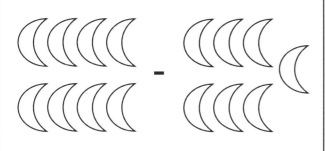

☐ - ☐ = ☐

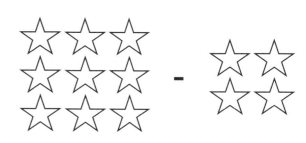

☐ - ☐ = ☐

Subtracting Using Pictures

Count and Subtract.

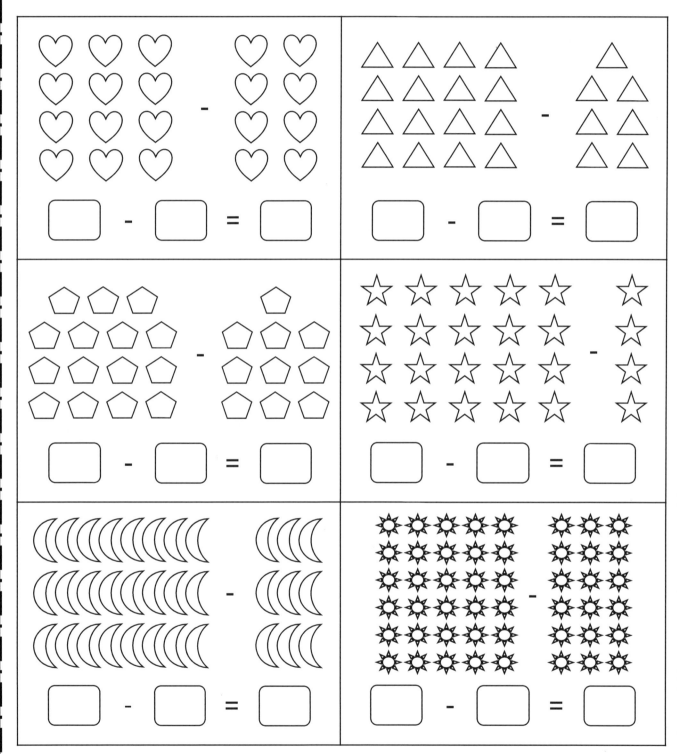

Find the difference.

3 - 2	4 - 1	5 - 3	6 - 2
5 - 1	4 - 3	6 - 1	3 - 3
7 - 1	8 - 1	9 - 3	7 - 2
8 - 3	9 - 4	8 - 2	9 - 2

Subtraction in Columns

Find the difference.

$\begin{array}{r} 7 \\ -\ 3 \\ \hline \end{array}$	$\begin{array}{r} 6 \\ -\ 5 \\ \hline \end{array}$	$\begin{array}{r} 8 \\ -\ 4 \\ \hline \end{array}$	$\begin{array}{r} 9 \\ -\ 0 \\ \hline \end{array}$
$\begin{array}{r} 8 \\ -\ 5 \\ \hline \end{array}$	$\begin{array}{r} 9 \\ -\ 5 \\ \hline \end{array}$	$\begin{array}{r} 7 \\ -\ 4 \\ \hline \end{array}$	$\begin{array}{r} 8 \\ -\ 8 \\ \hline \end{array}$
$\begin{array}{r} 8 \\ -\ 7 \\ \hline \end{array}$	$\begin{array}{r} 7 \\ -\ 5 \\ \hline \end{array}$	$\begin{array}{r} 9 \\ -\ 6 \\ \hline \end{array}$	$\begin{array}{r} 7 \\ -\ 0 \\ \hline \end{array}$
$\begin{array}{r} 9 \\ -\ 7 \\ \hline \end{array}$	$\begin{array}{r} 7 \\ -\ 6 \\ \hline \end{array}$	$\begin{array}{r} 8 \\ -\ 6 \\ \hline \end{array}$	$\begin{array}{r} 9 \\ -\ 8 \\ \hline \end{array}$

Subtraction in Columns

Find the difference.

14 - 2	15 - 3	17 - 4	19 - 1
22 - 2	26 - 5	38 - 6	44 - 4
59 - 6	67 - 5	78 - 3	85 - 4
99 - 7	88 - 1	79 - 8	57 - 2

Subtraction in Columns

Find the difference.

38 - 4	76 - 5	45 - 1	37 - 2
84 - 3	93 - 3	58 - 1	69 - 8
87 - 5	79 - 2	38 - 7	76 - 3
98 - 5	49 - 9	77 - 4	89 - 3

Subtraction in Columns

Find the difference.

14 - 10	36 - 13	15 - 11	27 - 12
43 - 23	56 - 51	48 - 32	69 - 41
47 - 25	85 - 34	68 - 35	57 - 17
99 - 20	67 - 10	78 - 52	89 - 11

Subtraction in Columns

Find the difference.

25 - 12	47 - 15	26 - 12	39 - 13
65 - 30	67 - 23	59 - 21	78 - 31
59 - 32	86 - 44	67 - 41	58 - 32
68 - 44	79 - 30	97 - 72	98 - 45

Mental Subtraction

Find the difference.

4 - 2 = ☐	6 - 2 = ☐
5 - 2 = ☐	6 - 1 = ☐
7 - 3 = ☐	8 - 2 = ☐
9 - 3 = ☐	7 - 2 = ☐
7 - 5 = ☐	8 - 3 = ☐
9 - 4 = ☐	6 - 6 = ☐
8 - 5 = ☐	9 - 2 = ☐
9 - 6 = ☐	8 - 7 = ☐

Mental Subtraction

Find the difference.

13 − 7 = ☐	27 − 3 = ☐
25 − 8 = ☐	15 − 4 = ☐
46 − 6 = ☐	66 − 9 = ☐
38 − 7 = ☐	74 − 5 = ☐
52 − 9 = ☐	67 − 7 = ☐
63 − 6 = ☐	85 − 9 = ☐
87 − 5 = ☐	91 − 4 = ☐
98 − 8 = ☐	72 − 9 = ☐

Mental Subtraction

Find the difference.

54 − 16 = ☐	19 − 13 = ☐
39 − 33 = ☐	42 − 21 = ☐
62 − 28 = ☐	73 − 29 = ☐
86 − 45 = ☐	96 − 47 = ☐
73 − 24 = ☐	69 − 49 = ☐
85 − 37 = ☐	78 − 52 = ☐
94 − 76 = ☐	87 − 11 = ☐
71 − 24 = ☐	90 − 12 = ☐

Mental Subtraction

Fill in the missing number.

$4 - \boxed{} = 1$	$6 - \boxed{} = 5$
$5 - \boxed{} = 3$	$9 - \boxed{} = 5$
$9 - \boxed{} = 2$	$8 - \boxed{} = 3$
$10 - \boxed{} = 4$	$9 - \boxed{} = 1$
$16 - \boxed{} = 7$	$14 - \boxed{} = 9$
$14 - \boxed{} = 8$	$12 - \boxed{} = 6$
$15 - \boxed{} = 7$	$16 - \boxed{} = 8$
$18 - \boxed{} = 9$	$17 - \boxed{} = 9$

Mental Subtraction

Fill in the missing number.

15 - ☐ = 11		18 - ☐ = 11
27 - ☐ = 18		35 - ☐ = 27
64 - ☐ = 59		47 - ☐ = 44
72 - ☐ = 66		83 - ☐ = 76
78 - ☐ = 70		31 - ☐ = 28
95 - ☐ = 86		80 - ☐ = 76
82 - ☐ = 77		57 - ☐ = 49
81 - ☐ = 72		90 - ☐ = 83

Mental Subtraction

Fill in the missing number.

36 - ☐ = 13	25 - ☐ = 14
59 - ☐ = 45	47 - ☐ = 36
81 - ☐ = 17	68 - ☐ = 34
72 - ☐ = 21	76 - ☐ = 23
83 - ☐ = 47	84 - ☐ = 56
64 - ☐ = 40	97 - ☐ = 77
57 - ☐ = 25	95 - ☐ = 38
78 - ☐ = 10	98 - ☐ = 12

Making Numbers

Think of five ways to make 3.

$$\boxed{} - \boxed{} = \boxed{3}$$

$$\boxed{} - \boxed{} = \boxed{3}$$

$$\boxed{} - \boxed{} = \boxed{3}$$

$$\boxed{} - \boxed{} - \boxed{} = \boxed{3}$$

$$\boxed{} - \boxed{} - \boxed{} = \boxed{3}$$

Think of five ways to make 4.

$$\boxed{} - \boxed{} - \boxed{} = \boxed{4}$$

$$\boxed{} - \boxed{} - \boxed{} = \boxed{4}$$

$$\boxed{} - \boxed{} - \boxed{} = \boxed{4}$$

$$\boxed{} - \boxed{} - \boxed{} = \boxed{4}$$

$$\boxed{} - \boxed{} - \boxed{} = \boxed{4}$$

Making Numbers

Think of five ways to make 5.

$\boxed{} - \boxed{} = \boxed{5}$

$\boxed{} - \boxed{} = \boxed{5}$

$\boxed{} - \boxed{} = \boxed{5}$

$\boxed{} - \boxed{} - \boxed{} = \boxed{5}$

$\boxed{} - \boxed{} - \boxed{} = \boxed{5}$

Think of five ways to make 6.

$\boxed{} - \boxed{} - \boxed{} = \boxed{6}$

$\boxed{} - \boxed{} - \boxed{} = \boxed{6}$

$\boxed{} - \boxed{} - \boxed{} = \boxed{6}$

$\boxed{} - \boxed{} - \boxed{} = \boxed{6}$

$\boxed{} - \boxed{} - \boxed{} = \boxed{6}$

Think of five ways to make 7.

☐ - ☐ = 7

☐ - ☐ = 7

☐ - ☐ = 7

☐ - ☐ - ☐ = 7

☐ - ☐ - ☐ = 7

Think of five ways to make 8.

☐ - ☐ - ☐ = 8

☐ - ☐ - ☐ = 8

☐ - ☐ - ☐ = 8

☐ - ☐ - ☐ = 8

☐ - ☐ - ☐ = 8

Making Numbers

Think of five ways to make 9.

$\boxed{} - \boxed{} = \boxed{9}$

$\boxed{} - \boxed{} = \boxed{9}$

$\boxed{} - \boxed{} = \boxed{9}$

$\boxed{} - \boxed{} - \boxed{} = \boxed{9}$

$\boxed{} - \boxed{} - \boxed{} = \boxed{9}$

Think of five ways to make 10.

$\boxed{} - \boxed{} - \boxed{} = \boxed{10}$

$\boxed{} - \boxed{} - \boxed{} = \boxed{10}$

$\boxed{} - \boxed{} - \boxed{} = \boxed{10}$

$\boxed{} - \boxed{} - \boxed{} = \boxed{10}$

$\boxed{} - \boxed{} - \boxed{} = \boxed{10}$

Subtraction Word Problems

Read and solve the problems.

1) You have eight cookies and you ate four of them. How many cookies do you have left?

2) There are seven birds and three nests. How many more birds are there than nests?

3) Sophia baked 11 boxes of cookies and 5 boxes of muffins. Then she sold 4 boxes of cookies. How many boxes of cookies were left?

Subtraction Word Problems

Read and solve the problems.

1) The team ordered 24 shirts and shorts for the players. However, 3 shirts shrunk, and 7 shorts were discolored. How many shirts and shorts are left?

2) Elijah found 4 small whiteboards and 7 boxes of markers for coaches to use. Oliver said they need a total of 13 whiteboards and 11 boxes of markers. How many more whiteboards and boxes of markers were needed?

3) James has a box of toy vehicles. There are 26 cars, 30 trucks and 42 emergency vehicles.15 cars are blue and 9 are white. The rest are red. How many red cars are there in the box?

Subtraction Word Problems

Read and solve the problems.

1) Jacob, Ben and Collin are building towers of blocks. Jacob uses 15 blocks. Ben uses 21 blocks. Collin uses 9 blocks. If there are 72 blocks in total, how many blocks are left?

2) Jack is making pictures with different shapes. He cuts out some triangles, squares and circles using red, green, and blue construction paper. He cut out 29 triangles, 25 squares and 12 circles. If there are 7 red triangles and the same number of blue triangles, how many green triangles are there?

3) Lucas told his teacher that she made a mistake correcting his math test. She gave him a mark of 18 out of 20. It should have been 13 out of 20. How many points must the teacher now take away?

Subtraction Word Problems

Read and solve the problems.

1) 51 students are going to the zoo. the students need to go in 3 groups. There are 20 students in the first group and 16 students in the second group. How many students are in the third group?

2) In the basketball arcade game, players need to get 70 points in one game to receive prizes. Partway through the game, Owen had 35 points and Samuel had 27 points. How many more points does Samuel need to receive a prize?

3) Linda's hair is 10 inches long. If her hair grows 3 more inches each month, how long will it be in three more months?

Mixed Addition and Subtraction

Add and Subtract.

$2 + 3 - 4 = \boxed{}$ $3 + 4 - 2 = \boxed{}$

$5 + 2 - 5 = \boxed{}$ $6 + 3 - 1 = \boxed{}$

$7 + 1 - 4 = \boxed{}$ $5 + 4 - 6 = \boxed{}$

$5 + 5 - 3 = \boxed{}$ $8 + 1 - 4 = \boxed{}$

$6 + 6 - 6 = \boxed{}$ $7 + 9 - 8 = \boxed{}$

$7 + 8 - 1 = \boxed{}$ $9 + 7 - 6 = \boxed{}$

$8 + 8 - 3 = \boxed{}$ $6 + 9 - 4 = \boxed{}$

$9 + 8 - 2 = \boxed{}$ $7 + 7 - 9 = \boxed{}$

Mixed Addition and Subtraction

Add and Subtract.

12 + 5 - 9 = ☐   15 + 8 - 13 = ☐

16 + 7 - 10 = ☐   25 + 9 - 17 = ☐

14 + 21 - 30 = ☐   34 + 20 - 18 = ☐

57 + 9 - 42 = ☐   45 + 22 - 36 = ☐

45 + 49 - 71 = ☐   80 + 19 - 50 = ☐

87 + 9 - 66 = ☐   74 + 13 - 81 = ☐

69 + 30 - 92 = ☐   82 + 18 - 53 = ☐

45 + 37 - 58 = ☐   77 + 23 - 85 = ☐

Mixed Addition and Subtraction

Read and solve the problems.

1) A string of lights has 17 light bulbs but 9 of them are broken. Jack only has 5 replacement bulbs. How many light bulbs are working?

2) On Thursday, 43 patients made appointments with Dr. Bloom and 14 patients did not show up. Also, 8 patients came in with no appointments. How many patients did Dr. Bloom have on Thursday?

3) Sean had fifty toy cars. If he gets twelve more cars and gives two to his little brother, how many cars will he have then?

Mixed Addition and Subtraction

Read and solve the problems.

1) Gabriel has 40 pencils. He gives 13 pencils to a friend. He buys 27 more pencils. How many pencils does Gabriel have now?

2) Lucy's mom baked 39 cookies. Brian's dad baked 26 cookies. Lucy and Brian ate 9 cookies each and then brought them to school for a party. How many cookies did they bring to school altogether?

3) 14 new lockers are delivered to the school but 6 of them come in the wrong size. The lockers with the right size are to be put on the first floor. Together with the old 3 lockers on the first floor, how many lockers are there in total on the 1st floor?

Mixed Addition and Subtraction

Read and solve the problems.

Asher, Isaac and Mila are keeping score of the game they are playing. When a player wins a game, that player gets 5 points. If a player loses a game, the player has 3 points taken away. If it is a tie, every player gets 2 points. Each of them has 20 points to start with. Asher wins the first game.

1) Isaac wins the second game. How many points does Isaac has after the second game? (remember to count the points Isaac gets for the first game!)

2) The third game is a tie. How many points does Mila have after the third game?

Mixed Addition and Subtraction

Read and solve the problems.

A bus leaves the terminal every morning at 7 o'clock.
There are 30 seats on the left side of the bus and 26 seats on the right side. When the bus left the terminal this morning, 8 passengers sat on the bus. At the first stop, 17 passengers got on the bus.

1) At the second stop, 13 passengers get on the bus and 11 got off. How many passengers were there on the bus?

2) There were 5 less passengers getting on at the third stop than the second stop. 4 passengers got off at the third stop. How many passengers were there on the bus after the 3rd stop?

Game and Challenge

Fill in the missing numbers to complete the sums.

$$20 - \bigcirc = 7$$

$$+ \quad - \quad +$$

$$\bigcirc + 10 = \bigcirc$$

$$= \quad = \quad =$$

$$\bigcirc - \bigcirc = 19$$

$$\bigcirc - \bigcirc = 4$$

$$+ \quad - \quad +$$

$$\bigcirc + 8 = \bigcirc$$

$$= \quad = \quad =$$

$$27 - \bigcirc = 20$$

Fill in the missing numbers to complete the sums.

$$30 - (\ \ ) = 14$$

30	−	( )	=	14
+		−		+
( )	+	14	=	( )
=		=		=
( )	−	( )	=	28

( )	−	20	=	( )
+		−		+
20	+	( )	=	( )
=		=		=
40	−	( )	=	30

Game and Challenge

Use your math skills to find the value of each "?".

🐔 = [?]   🦉 = [?]

🦔 − 🐟 = 10

🐟 + 🐟 − 🦔 = 0

🦔 = [?]   🐟 = [?]

Game and Challenge

Use your math skills to find the value of each "?".

🐸 + 🐓 + 🐓 = 27

🐸 + 🐸 = 14

🐓 - 🕷 = 5

🐓 = [?]

🕷 = [?]

🐸 = [?]

66

Use your math skills to find the value of each "?".

△ + 2 = ☽

☽ - 9 = ★

18 - ★ = ♡

♡ + 4 = 15

☽ = [?]   △ = [?]

♡ = [?]   ★ = [?]

Game and Challenge

Use your math skills to find the value of each "?".

$$\star + \star - \text{(cylinder)} = \boxed{34}$$

$$\star - \heartsuit = \boxed{10}$$

$$\text{(moon)} = \boxed{32\text{-}21\text{+}6}$$

$$\text{(cylinder)} + \text{(moon)} = \boxed{21}$$

(moon) = ? $\star$ = ?

(cylinder) = ? $\heartsuit$ = ?

Game and Challenge

Use your math skills to find the value of each "?".

 + 9 =

 − 5 =

 + 6 =

 + 3 = 7

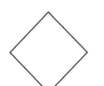 = [?]   = [?]

 = [?]   = [?]

69

Game and Challenge

Use your math skills to find the value of each "?".

$$\star + \heartsuit + \star = \text{cylinder}$$

$$25 - \text{cylinder} = \text{moon}$$

$$\text{moon} + \text{moon} = 10$$

$$\star + \star = \text{moon} + 9$$

$$\text{cylinder} - \heartsuit = \boxed{?}$$

$$\text{moon} = \boxed{?} \qquad \star = \boxed{?}$$

$$\text{cylinder} = \boxed{?} \qquad \heartsuit = \boxed{?}$$

Game and Challenge

Use your math skills to find the value of each "?".

+ + + = 31

19 = +

+ − 3 = 13

30 − = 18

= ?

= ?

= ?

= ?

Game and Challenge

Use your math skills to find the value of each "?".

 + + = 24

 - 3 + = 19

5 = -

 - 7 =

 +  -  = ?

 = ?

 = ?

= ?

= ?

72

Game and Challenge

Use your math skills to find the value of each "?".

🍊 + 🍎 + 🍊 = 28

30 = 🍇 + 🍇 + 🪑

🪑 = 🍇

🍎 = 🪑 - 6

🍎 + 🪑 + 🍊 + 🍇 = ?

🍎 = ?   🍇 = ?

🪑 = ?   🍊 = ?

Comparing Numbers

Compare with >,< or =.

0 ◯ 0   5 ◯ 4

3 ◯ 2   6 ◯ 7

7 ◯ 9   8 ◯ 5

9 ◯ 15   16 ◯ 19

11 ◯ 10   13 ◯ 20

10 ◯ 20   56 ◯ 7

73 ◯ 9   81 ◯ 6

8 ◯ 48   9 ◯ 9

Comparing Numbers

Compare with >,< or =.

26 ◯ 33   42 ◯ 61

57 ◯ 58   72 ◯ 22

43 ◯ 19   50 ◯ 49

29 ◯ 49   51 ◯ 15

80 ◯ 77   69 ◯ 48

88 ◯ 90   71 ◯ 59

33 ◯ 64   89 ◯ 91

87 ◯ 77   97 ◯ 99

Ordering Numbers

Arrange these numbers in order, from least to greatest.

a. 5, 9, 8, 3	____ < ____ < ____ < ____
b. 7, 4, 8, 6	____ < ____ < ____ < ____
c. 1, 0, 2, 5	____ < ____ < ____ < ____
d. 9, 7, 3, 2	____ < ____ < ____ < ____
e. 10, 13, 5, 9	____ < ____ < ____ < ____
f. 6, 17, 7, 0	____ < ____ < ____ < ____
g. 8, 20, 14, 15	____ < ____ < ____ < ____
h. 11, 9, 19, 16	____ < ____ < ____ < ____
i. 18, 3, 8, 12	____ < ____ < ____ < ____

Ordering Numbers

Arrange these numbers in order, from least to greatest.

a. 29, 57, 8, 11	____ < ____ < ____ < ____
b. 45, 36, 16, 69	____ < ____ < ____ < ____
c. 71, 50, 42, 30	____ < ____ < ____ < ____
d. 17, 65, 4, 37	____ < ____ < ____ < ____
e. 44, 34, 84, 74	____ < ____ < ____ < ____
f. 82, 73, 90, 15	____ < ____ < ____ < ____
g. 30, 91, 89, 67	____ < ____ < ____ < ____
h. 83, 60, 50, 70	____ < ____ < ____ < ____
i. 100, 99, 86, 79	____ < ____ < ____ < ____

Measurement

Answer the question by circling the correct picture.

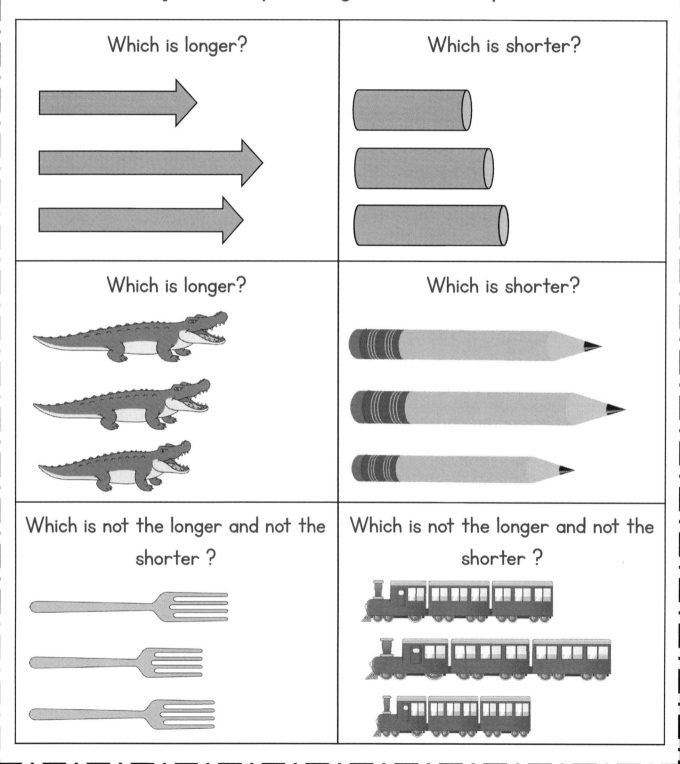

Which is longer?

Which is shorter?

Which is longer?

Which is shorter?

Which is not the longer and not the shorter ?

Which is not the longer and not the shorter ?

Measurement

Use a ruler to measure this objects.

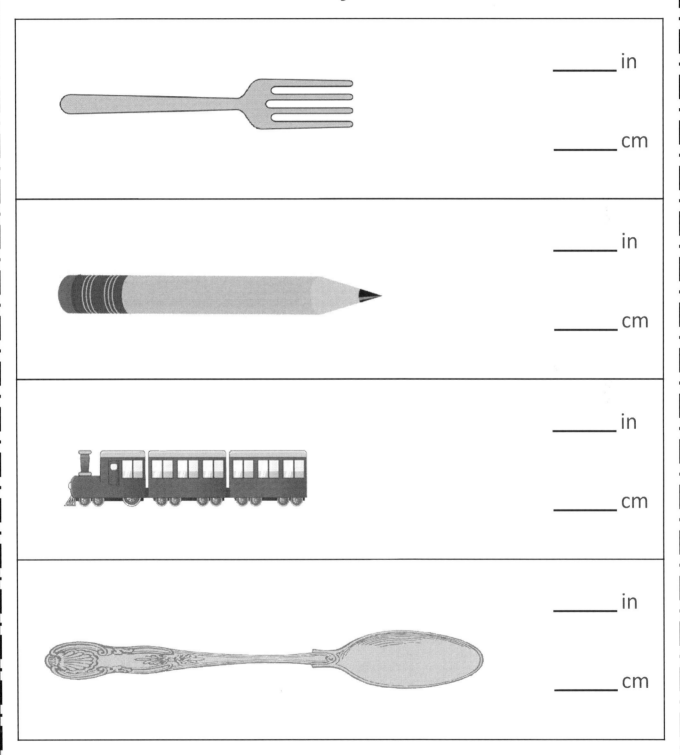

_____ in

_____ cm

_____ in

_____ cm

_____ in

_____ cm

_____ in

_____ cm

Measurement

Use a ruler to measure this objects.

_____ in

_____ cm

_____ in

_____ cm

_____ in

_____ cm

_____ in

_____ cm

Measurement

Answer the question by coloring the correct picture.

Color the heaviest animal.	Color the lightest fruits.
Color the heaviest object.	Color the lightest vehicle.
Color the animal that is not the heaviest and not the lightest.	Color the object that is not the heaviest and not the lightest

Measurement

Match the proper unit of measurement with the objects.

OUNCES   POUNDS   TONS

Measurement

Match the proper unit of measurement with the objects.

OUNCES   POUNDS   TONS

   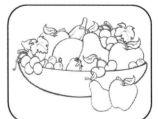

Measurement

Match the proper unit of measurement with the objects.

GRAMS   KILOGRAMS

  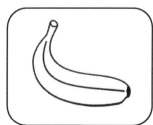 

Measurement

Match the proper unit of measurement with the objects.

GRAMS   KILOGRAMS

Game and Challenge

Use your math skills to find the value of each "?".

Game and Challenge

Use your math skills to find the value of each "?".

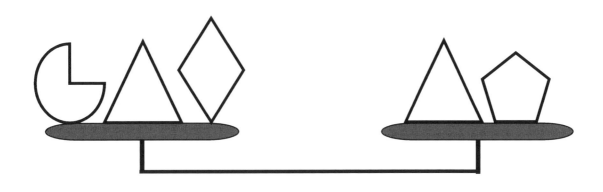

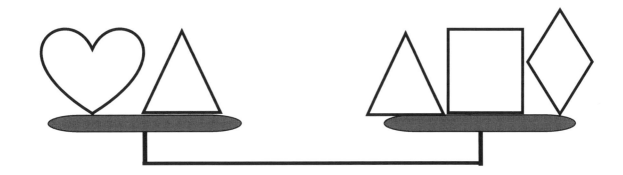

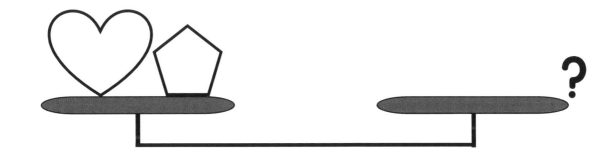

Game and Challenge

Use your math skills to find the value of each "?".

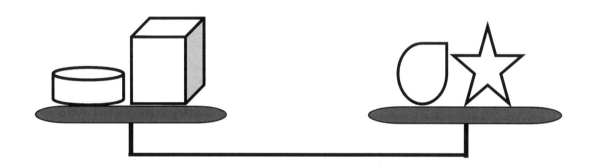

Game and Challenge

Use your math skills to find the value of each "?".

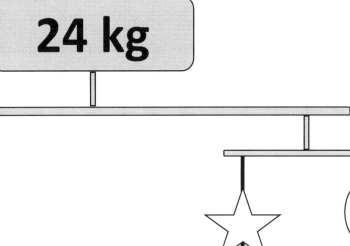

24 kg

 = ?

 = ?

 = ?

 = ?

Game and Challenge

Use your math skills to find the value of each "?".

32 kg

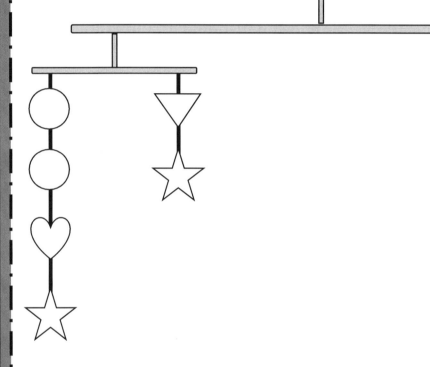
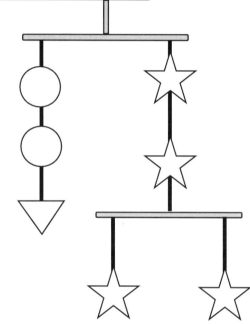

♡ = [?]   ◯ = [?]

☆ = [?]   ▽ = [?]

You are doing some gardening, and need exactly 4 liters of water to mix up some special formula for your award winning roses.

But you only have a 5-liter and a 3-liter bowl, but do have access to plenty of water.

How would you measure exactly 4 liters?

5-liter   3-liter

Fractions : Equal Parts

Mark the shapes that have been split into equal parts.

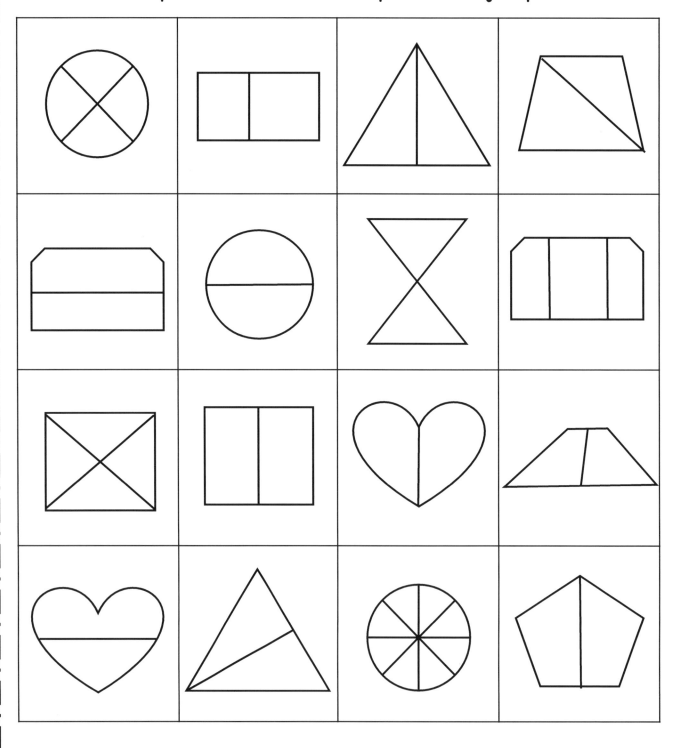

Reading Fractions

Draw a line to match the fraction to the words.

One half	$\dfrac{2}{3}$
One third	$\dfrac{4}{5}$
One quarter	$\dfrac{1}{4}$
Two thirds	$\dfrac{8}{9}$
Three quarters	$\dfrac{1}{2}$
Four quarters	$\dfrac{3}{6}$
Four fifth	$\dfrac{1}{3}$
Three sixth	$\dfrac{4}{4}$
Seven eighth	$\dfrac{3}{4}$
Eight nineth	$\dfrac{7}{8}$

Numerator and Denominator

Fill in the table.

Fraction		Numerator	Denominator
$\dfrac{1}{2}$			
$\dfrac{2}{3}$			
$\dfrac{3}{4}$			
$\dfrac{5}{7}$			
$\dfrac{4}{8}$			

Numerator and Denominator

Fill in the table.

Fraction		Numerator	Denominator
	★★☆☆☆	2	5
	★☆☆☆	1	4
	♥♥♥♥♥♥	3	6
	●●●○●●●●	7	8
	♥♥♥♥♥♥♥♥♥	4	9

Coloring to Make Fractions

Color in the fraction shown of each shape.

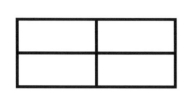 $\dfrac{2}{4}$ 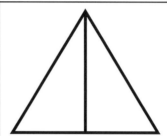 $\dfrac{1}{2}$

 $\dfrac{3}{4}$  $\dfrac{2}{3}$

 $\dfrac{5}{8}$ 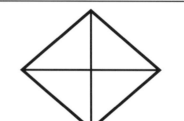 $\dfrac{4}{4}$

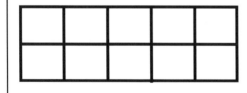 $\dfrac{6}{10}$ 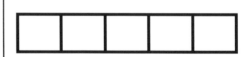 $\dfrac{3}{5}$

 $\dfrac{7}{8}$ 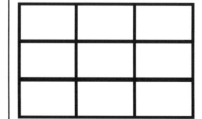 $\dfrac{4}{9}$

Coloring to Make Fractions

Color in the fraction shown of each shape.

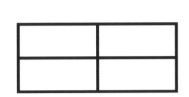 $\dfrac{1}{4}$

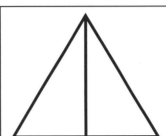 $\dfrac{2}{2}$

 $\dfrac{0}{4}$

 $\dfrac{1}{3}$

 $\dfrac{3}{8}$

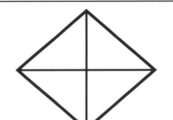 $\dfrac{2}{4}$

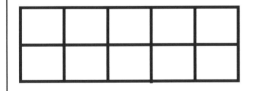 $\dfrac{9}{10}$

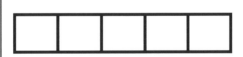 $\dfrac{1}{5}$

 $\dfrac{4}{8}$

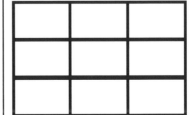 $\dfrac{8}{9}$

Writing Fractions

What fraction of the hearts are black? ____

What fraction of the triangles are black? ____

What fraction of the arrows point up? ____

What fraction of the cercles are black? ____

What fraction of the pentagons are black? ____

What fraction of the stars are black? ____

What fraction of the moons are black? ____

What fraction of the squares are black? ____

Writing Fractions

What fraction of the hearts are black? ____

What fraction of the triangles are black? ____

What fraction of the arrows point up? ____

What fraction of the cercles are black? ____

What fraction of the pentagons are black? ____

What fraction of the stars are black? ____

What fraction of the moons are black? ____

What fraction of the squares are black? ____

Fractions Word Problems

Read and answer each question.

There are 9 cars in the parking lot. 2 cars are parked on the left and the other cars are parked on the right.

1. What fraction of the cars are parked on the right?

2. If 4 cars are white, what fraction of the cars are white?

3. If 2 cars are sportscars, what fraction of the cars are sportscars?

4. If $\frac{5}{9}$ of the cars are minivans, how many minivans are there?

5. During lunch time, $\frac{3}{9}$ of the cars left the parking lot. How many cars are left?

Fractions Word Problems

Read and answer each question.

There are 24 students in a class. 11 of them are girls.

1. What fraction of the class are girls?

2. What fraction of the class are boys?

3. If 15 students ordered orange juice, what fraction of the class ordered orange juice?

4. If $\frac{10}{24}$ of students brings pizza for lunch, how many students have pizza for lunch?

5. $\frac{19}{24}$ of the students bring their parent consent forms for their field trip. How many of the students have not brought in their forms?

Read and answer each question.

Olivia is cleaning her dresser. She had three piles of clothing: shirts, pants, and skirts. She has 16 shirts, 8 pairs of pants and 5 skirts.

1. What fraction of the clothing are shirts?

2. If $\frac{3}{8}$ of the pants are jeans, how many pairs of jeans are there?

3. If $\frac{5}{16}$ of the shirts are white and $\frac{7}{16}$ are blue, are there more blue shirts or more white shirts?

4. If the rest of the shirts are black, how many black shirts are there?

5. Her mom brings 2 more shirts to her from the laundry. What is the new fraction of the clothing that are pants?

Telling Time

Draw the time shown on each clock.

1.

2:00

2.

4:30

3.

7:35

4.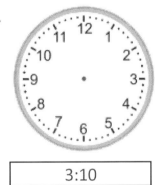

3:10

5.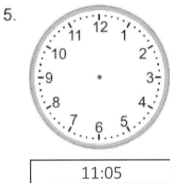

11:05

6.

9:45

7.

8:00

8.

12:00

9.

12:30

Telling Time

Draw the time shown on each clock.

1.

7:15

2.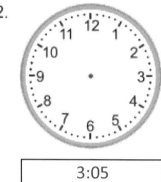

3:05

3.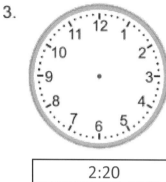

2:20

4.

6:45

5.

8:10

6.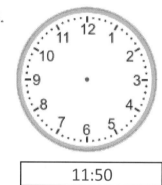

11:50

7.

12:40

8.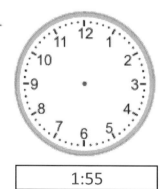

1:55

9.

10:25

Elapsed Time

Read and answer each question.

What time will it be in 1 hour 0 minutes?

What time will it be in 3 hours 0 minutes?

What time was it 4 hours 0 minutes ago?

What time was it 5 hours 30 minutes ago?

What time will it be in 4 hours 45 minutes?

What time was it 2 hours 5 minutes ago?

Elapsed Time

Read and answer each question.

What time will it be in 3 hour 45 minutes?

What time will it be in 4 hours 5 minutes?

What time was it 2 hours 20 minutes ago?

What time was it 1 hours 10 minutes ago?

What time will it be in 6 hours 15 minutes?

What time was it 4 hours 35 minutes ago?

Units of Time

Circle the best estimate of the time needed for each activity.

Sleeping at night.

Hours   Minutes   Seconds

Switching on the computer.

Weeks   Minutes   Seconds

Fixing a road.

Days   Minutes   Seconds

Taking a nap in the afternoon.

2 hours   2 minutes   2 seconds

Getting dressed for school.

4 minutes   4 years   4 seconds

Units of Time

Circle the best estimate of the time needed for each activity.

Having Christmas break from school.

2 weeks   2 minutes   2 hours

Taking a picture.

Hours   Minutes   Seconds

Taking a morning jog.

20 months   20 minutes   20 seconds

Building a new bridge.

3 days   3 months   3 minutes

Building a new apartment building.

1 week   1 seconds   1 year

AM & PM

Does this happen in the a.m. or p.m.?

Postman delivering mail in the morning	→	A. M. / P. M.
Playing toys after dinner	→	A. M. / P. M.
Stargazing	→	A. M. / P. M.
Birthday party on a Saturday morning	→	A. M. / P. M.
Rooster crowing at dawn	→	A. M. / P. M.
Riding bike after lunch	→	A. M. / P. M.
Taking school bus to school	→	A. M. / P. M.

Converting Time

Convert the time.

1 min = _____ seconds

1 hour = _____ minutes

1 day = _____ hours

1 week = _____ days

1 month = _____ days

1 year = _____ days

1 year = _____ months

1 month = _____ weeks

Identifying Shapes

Write the name of each shape using the following words.

Rhombus   Sphere   Cercle   Rectangle   Square

Parallelogram   Triangle   Cone

Trapezoid   Hexagon   Oval   Pentagon

(pentagon)	(rhombus)	(trapezoid)
(square)	(circle)	(hexagon)
(triangle)	(parallelogram)	(rectangle)

Identifying Shapes

Write the name of each shape using the following words.

Sphere   Pyramid   Cone   Star   Rectangle
   Triangle
Cube   Cuboid   Hexagonal Prism   Cylinder
   Oval   Rhombus

112

Sides and Vertices

Count how many sides and vertices for each shape.

Shape	Number of Sides	Number of Vertices

Sides and Vertices

Count how many sides and vertices for each shape.

Shape	Number of Sides	Number of Vertices
(oval)		
(square)		
(hexagon)		
(star)		
(pentagon)		
(cube)		

Perimeter of 2D Shapes

Find the perimeter of the shapes shown below.

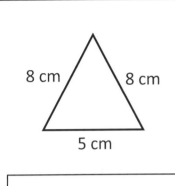

8 cm   8 cm

5 cm

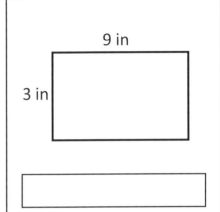

3 m

3 m   3 m

3 m

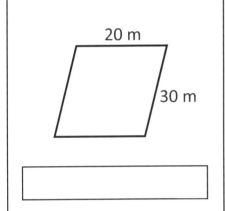

9 in

3 in

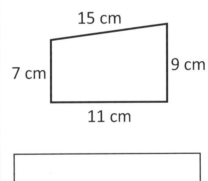

20 m

30 m

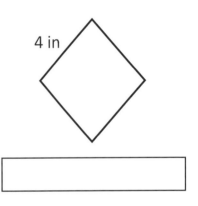

15 cm

7 cm   9 cm

11 cm

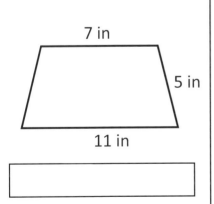

4 in

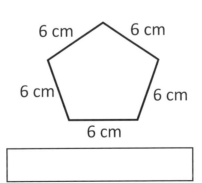

7 in

5 in

11 in

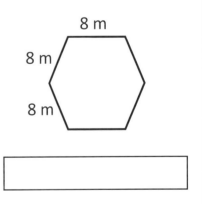

6 cm   6 cm

6 cm   6 cm

6 cm

8 m

8 m

8 m

115

Symmetry of 2D Shapes

Draw a line that cuts the following shapes in half, so that each half reflects the other half through your line.
Hint: Some shapes can be cut in more than one way.

Symmetry of 2D Shapes

Drawing the other half of the following symmetric shapes.

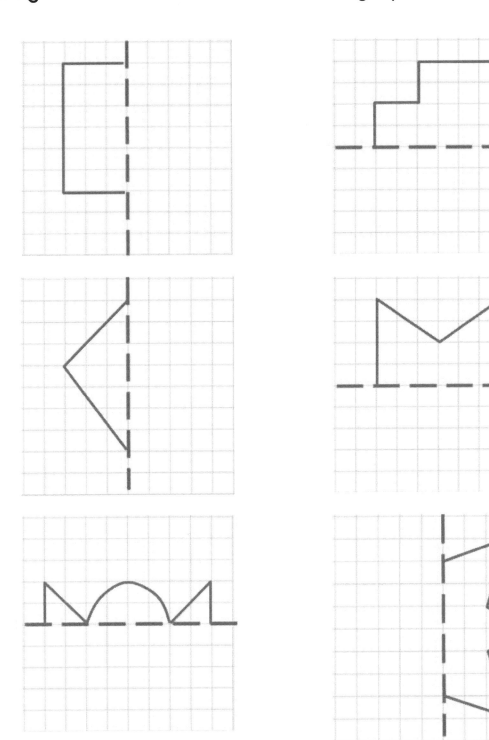

Symmetry of 2D Shapes

Drawing the other half of the following symmetric shapes.

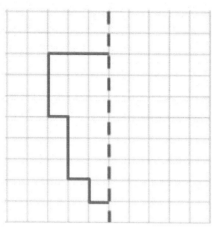
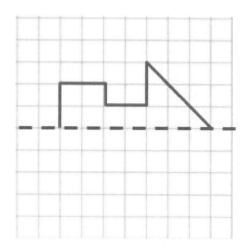
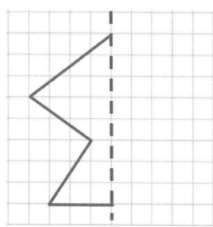
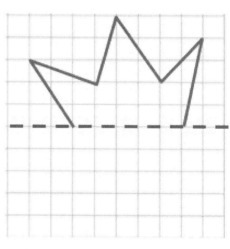
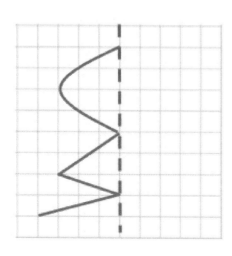
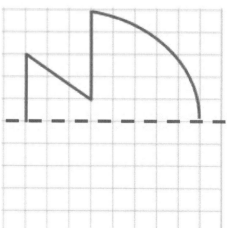

Game and Challenge

Drawing the other half of this symmetric rocket.

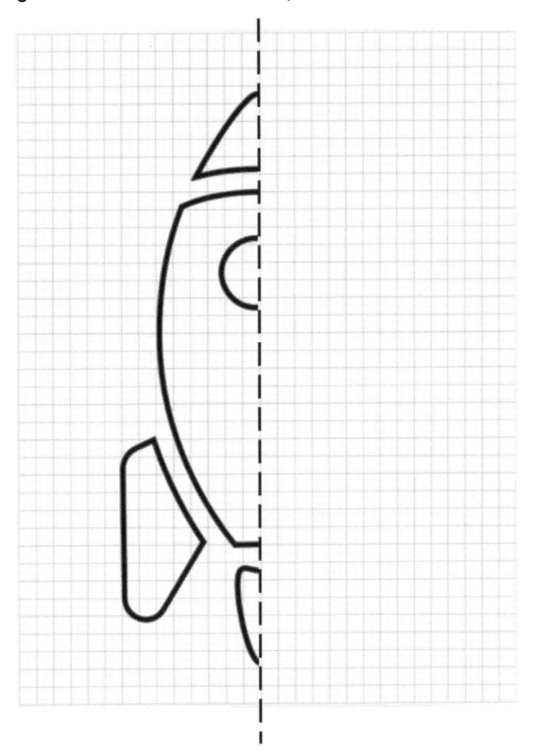

Drawing the other half of this symmetric bug.

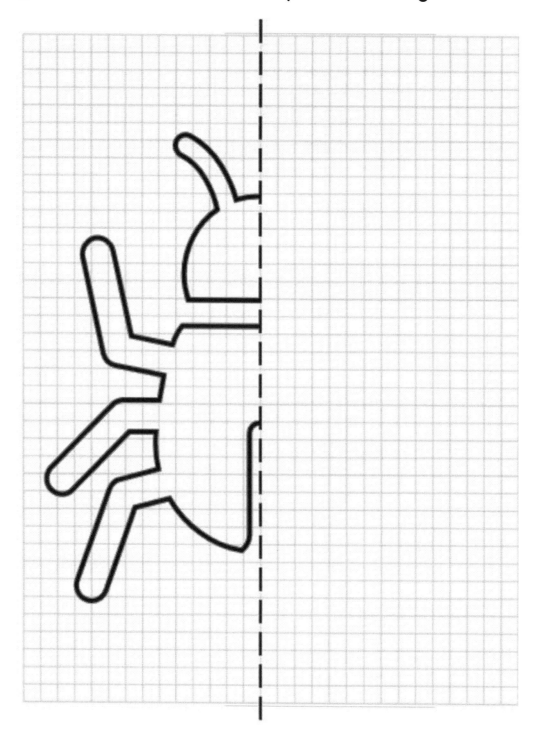

Made in the USA
Coppell, TX
15 October 2024

38714416R00068